Traveling on the Number Nine Bus

Nonet Poems

Traveling on the Number Nine Bus

Nonet Poems by

Fran Abrams

© 2025 Fran Abrams. All rights reserved.
This material may not be reproduced in any form, published,
reprinted, recorded, performed, broadcast,
rewritten, or redistributed without
the explicit permission of Fran Abrams.
All such actions are strictly prohibited by law.

Cover design by Shay Culligan
Cover image by Bobby Donovan
Untitled, Oil on canvas, 17-1/8" x 21-1/8"
From the private collection of Darick Allen
Cover image photographed by Emily Tellez
Author photograph by Jaree Donnelly

ISBN: 978-1-63980-986-8

Kelsay Books
502 South 1040 East, A-119
American Fork, Utah 84003
Kelsaybooks.com

A collection of
Nonet and reverse Nonet poems

A Nonet is a nine-line poem with nine syllables in the first line, eight syllables in the second line, seven syllables in the third line continuing through one syllable in the ninth line. A reverse Nonet has one syllable in the first line, two syllables in the second line, three syllables in the third line continuing through nine syllables in the ninth line.

Contents

I. People on the Bus

It's crowded but mostly the same folks	15
"Let me off, let me off," yells a voice	16
She thinks she	17
Rainy days are dreadful for riding	18
Bus wheezes	19
The ladies who lunch wear fancy hats	20
Since they made it free for students	21

II. She Drives the Bus

Many times Jenn wonders why	25
The days Jenn likes least are when it snows	26
Stop she likes best is outside movie	27
Jenn is not a fan of blood, mainly	28
Every time Jenn drives across the bridge	29
Jenn never speaks of days off when she	30
At Christmas time, Jenn hands out red	31
Deciding what to wear is always	32
When she takes her break at each end	33
Jenn goes home each evening to black cat	34

III. Secrets on the Bus

Watch that man	37
He thinks we don't notice his Friday	38
Kay is planning to elope instead	39
Meg never tells anyone she	40
Lines showed up pink. There was no boyfriend	41

The secrets on the number nine bus   42
Mrs. Cohn insists the man sitting   43
She called herself Annie when she said   44
Beth rarely speaks to other riders   45
Brett has a good secret she can't share   46

IV. Where the Bus Stops

There are days when there are more shopping   49
Route nine runs along the northern edge   50
It's a pleasant surprise to find a   51
Bus nine stops at town's railroad station   52
Not surprising our town's history   53
Home of town office, court house, and jail   54
Much to everybody's shock, a big   55
Library sits on wooded hillside.   56
Large subdivision of new homes built   57
If you're looking for a town to love   58

I. People on the Bus

It's crowded but mostly the same folks
each day, although you may not know
their names. Woman in knit hat,
its color changing with
seasons, pink in spring,
tan in fall. You
notice when
she's not
there.

"Let me off, let me off," yells a voice
from the rear of the bus, someone
frightened they had missed their stop.
Brakes squeal, standing riders
sway, hang onto poles.
Normal sound track
of number
nine bus.
Noise.

She
thinks she
knows you from
riding bus nine
at busy rush hour,
times when riders are packed
tighter than posts in stockade
fences as they try not to get
personal with elbows and handbags.

Rainy days are dreadful for riding
the bus because anyone who
might have walked that day now wants
to ride on the dry bus.
They stand together
wearing wet coats
and fling drops
through the
air.

Bus
wheezes,
stops in front
of shiny stone
building with door man.
Bus passenger walks to
door with aplomb as if he
has just alighted from limo,
confident as he begins his day.

The ladies who lunch wear fancy hats
as they ride the bus downtown to
their favorite restaurant,
sip an alcoholic
drink or three, return
safely home by
bus without
driving
drunk.

Since they made it free for students to
ride buses, traveling when school
day ends has become a trip
to avoid. Big high school
students use bodies
and book bags like
unguided
missiles.
Ouch.

II. She Drives the Bus

Many times Jenn wonders why she is
a bus operator—formal
name for her work. She's always
liked engines and people,
an unusual
combination.
Turns out, it's
a great
job.

The days Jenn likes least are when it snows.
Yes, buses need to be running
although if there is too much
snow, updates tell riders
route will skip small streets.
Walk to large streets.
She'll offer
boarding
there.

Stop she likes best is outside movie
theater where patrons coming or
going are sure to discuss
the movie they will see
or have seen. Jenn hears
about bad jokes
and bloody
murder
scenes.

Jenn is not a fan of blood, mainly
when it is someone on her bus
bleeding. She knows there can be
fights, how to call cops. It
makes her mad other
riders have to
walk or wait
for next
bus.

Every time Jenn drives across the bridge,
she tries not to look down at churn
of river, recalls stories
she's read about bridges
crumpling. She does not
want to become
the one who
takes a
dive.

Jenn never speaks of days off when she
rides bus nine driven by someone
else. She likes to visit her
favorite Dim Sum place
on Ninth to drink tea
and relax in
a booth that
does not
move.

At Christmas time, Jenn hands out red and
white striped sweets. She wears a red cap,
wishes her riders joyous
holidays. It is how
she finds her good mood.
She earns extra
working more.
Joy to
her.

Deciding what to wear is always
a challenge. Jenn has lightweight and
heavy uniforms, too. Long
underwear helps on the
coldest of days. When
it's hot, she must
rely on
fan in
bus.

When she takes her break at each end of
her route, she always listens to
news. She knows if big story
is brewing, she'll want to
keep up to date so
she can say, "Yes"
when they ask
if she's
heard.

Jenn goes home each evening to black cat
named *Michelin* after tires
on her bus. Cat's preferred stunt
is whirling in circles
as if mimicking
spinning wheels. At
day's end, cat
makes her
laugh.

III. Secrets on the Bus

Watch
that man
getting off
the bus at Twelfth
and Summit who looks
around until he sees
a florist shop and enters
while we wonder what misdeed he
will be forgiven with a bouquet.

He thinks we don't notice his Friday
routine when he will disembark
at the Upperton Hotel,
that we do not suspect
someone waits for him
in a lavish
room for two
staged for
love.

Kay is planning to elope instead
of hosting a huge wedding. No
one knows except her maid of
honor and fiancé.
She shows her ring to
her friends on bus,
delights them
with her
news.

Meg never tells anyone she was
born in this town. Embarrassed her
Dad left. Mom raised her alone.
She went to college far
away. Tells friends she's
a new neighbor
here. Now town
welcomes
her.

Lines showed up pink. There was no boyfriend
to tell. He had abandoned her.
She's always wanted a child,
has told her bus nine friends
she'll make it somehow.
Soon her secret
will show for
all to
see.

The secrets on the number nine bus
are not very easy to see—
like Mrs. Kay's blonde wig, a
blue handkerchief Stanley
wears, and small stolen
pills hidden so
carefully
in Joan's
purse.

Mrs. Cohn insists the man sitting
in fourth row is a good friend of
a gangster, that he'll murder
your husband for the right
price. Her friends say that's
rubbish, but how
can they be
truly
sure?

She called herself Annie when she said,
"Hello" to new friends on bus. Just
arrived, got a job, did not
say she was hiding in
witness protection.
Must remember
to answer
to new
name.

Beth rarely speaks to other riders,
keeps her life to herself, does not
say she has four-year-old son
who stays with her mother
while she works downtown.
Divorce was hard.
Now they are
doing
fine.

Brett has a good secret she can't share
yet. She's been accepted to play
on *Jeopardy.* Show will tape
in March, air in July.
Secret now, although
one day, many
will see her
live on
screen.

IV. Where the Bus Stops

There are days when there are more shopping
bags than people on bus seats, bags
with logos from stores along
route. Driver knows the way
to the best deals in
town and frequent
riders know
where to
shop.

Route nine runs along the northern edge
of Chinatown, past restaurants
and stores with exotic wares.
Open bus window and
inhale aroma
of spicy soup
and bok choy.
Come for
lunch.

It's a pleasant surprise to find a
large lake in the midst of a park
downtown among dense buildings.
Ride on bus nine to edge
of park, walk to lake
and breathe as if
city's not
very
close.

Bus nine stops at town's railroad station—
easiest way to leave this town.
Someone boarding the bus with
a suitcase is likely
getting on a train.
It's friendly to
ask, "Where you
headed
to?"

Not surprising our town's history
museum sits next door to train
station. Both are historic,
quite old. Take nine bus to
visit museum.
Entry is free,
and you'll learn
something
new.

Home of town office, court house, and jail,
Town Square is heavily used stop.
Pay your tickets, look for deeds,
file animal control
complaint. A quiet
place until town's
newspaper
tells the
tales.

Much to everybody's shock, a big
box hardware store opened in town
where a department store had
closed. Now if you need a
hammer or drill, bus
nine gets you there.
Please no boards
on board
bus.

Library sits on wooded hillside.
Bus stop added when library
was rebuilt on land given
by founding family.
Attractive in all
seasons, pleasant
setting for
reading
books.

Large subdivision of new homes built
on Highway 14 near the bridge.
Bus stops there on winding route.
Homeowners are learning
it's great not to drive.
Bus gets you on
time where you
need to
go.

If you're looking for a town to love
with friendly people, too, I must
suggest you come visit us
and see it for yourself.
Be sure to ride the
number nine bus—
this town will
call to
you.

About the Author

Fran Abrams lives in Rockville, MD. She holds an undergraduate degree in art and architecture and a master's degree in urban planning. She retired in 2010 after 41 years of working in government and nonprofit agencies in Montgomery County, MD. Her work included a substantial amount of writing, including legislation, regulations, guidelines, reports, and other bureaucratic essentials.

In 2016, she realized how much she missed expressing herself in words and decided she wanted to write poetry, a form that was completely different from her past work. She attended a poetry reading early in 2017 and began taking poetry writing classes at The Writer's Center in Bethesda, MD, which she found enjoyable and encouraging.

Fran's poems are published online and in print in *The Delmarva Review, The Orchards Poetry Journal, Cathexis-Northwest Press, MacQueen's Quinterly Literary Magazine, The Raven's Perch, The Write Launch, Gargoyle,* and many others. They also appear in more than twenty anthologies, including the 2021 collection titled *This Is What America Looks Like* from Washington Writers Publishing House (WWPH).

Her full-length autobiographical book of poems is *I Rode the Second Wave: A Feminist Memoir* (Atmosphere Press, 2022). Her chapbooks are *The Poet Who Loves Pythagoras* (Finishing Line Press, 2023) and *Arranging Words* (Quillkeepers Press, 2023). This collection is her fourth book of poems. Fran also was one of four editors of a collection of poems, including her own, titled *Echoes Through the Stacks*, published in April 2024 by a group of poets who workshop their poems together at Quince Orchard Library in Gaithersburg, MD.

She has been a featured reader at DiVerse Gaithersburg (MD) Poetry Reading in 2021 and 2023 and read at the Gaithersburg Book Festival in May 2023.

For more, please visit:
franabramspoetry.com

www.ingramcontent.com/pod-product-compliance
Lightning Source LLC
Chambersburg PA
CBHW030915170426
43193CB00009BA/857